THE CIVI
IN YORKSHIRE

AN ACCOUNT OF THE BATTLES AND SIEGES AND YORKSHIRES INVOLVEMENT

COMPILED & WRITTEN

BY

KEITH SNOWDEN

CASTLEDEN PUBLICATIONS
PICKERING

ISBN 0-9514657-6-7

First published 1993
Reprinted 1993
Reprinted 1994
Reprinted 1995
Reprinted 1997
New impression 1998
Reprinted 1998
Reprinted 1999

Typeset, Printed & Bound
at the press of the publisher
CASTLEDEN PUBLICATIONS.
11, Castlegate, Pickering, North Yorkshire,
YO18 7AX. Telephone 01751 476227

INTRODUCTION

AS I write it has been estimated by a correspondent in a national newspaper that there are forty wars in progress on this planet at the present time, and that most of them are civil wars. If, like myself, the reader believes that war is a state of Hell on Earth, then a civil war must be a deeper recess of that hell, with kinsmen fighting each other. It is 350 years since the Civil War swept through Britain, and although present-day weaponry is more sophisticated, the treatment meted out to the victims of todays indigenous conflicts is no less merciless than that of previous centuries.

Also, as this book was being prepared for the press, the Royal Family was undergoing a series of crices, throwing some doubt on the prospect of there ever being a third King Charles, with the separation of the Wales'.

We can, perhaps, draw a parallel with the Charles of this book, whose Henrietta Maria, being a Roman Catholic, was classed as 'queen consort', for she refused to be crowned.

Much of the information given in the following pages has been derived from reports published well over one hundred years ago. This volume is intended to fill a gap, as I am given to understand by a member of a Civil War society that there is no book on the conflict in Yorkshire.

K.S.

Pickering,

March,1993.

P.S.

Since this book was first published it has proved to be very popular. Sadly events in the Royal family have taken an even more tragic turn and, unfortunately the number of wars presently raging increased to over fifty.

K.S.

1998.

To Ken, who gave me
the idea for this book.

PRELUDE TO WAR

THERE have been two main reasons given for the Civil War, namely taxation and religion. We can add a third, the intransigence of the king. At that time the king was required to defray the expenses of government. Charles I found this difficult to maintain from his income as Parliament was unsympathetic towards him and his policies. Charles began to raise money the best way he could ; he started selling titles. Sir Thomas Fairfax of Denton bought the title of Baron Fairfax of Cameron for £1,500. Manorial rights were sold at Almondsbury, Bainbridge, Bradford and Leeds. Hull had to pay £330.13s 4d as a forced loan. The king's father had started an early form of nationalisation by taking over the alum works founded by Sir Thomas Chaloner at Guisborough. One of the taxes that brought matters to a head was the £12,000 'Ship Money' demanded from Yorkshire.

Charles believed that the monarch ruled through Divine Providence and that he could do no wrong. His relations with Parliament became difficult and some of the members planned to emigrate to America, including Oliver Cromwell, but the king was fearful that they would help to widen the breach that already existed between the colonies and the English Church.

Some of the Pilgrim Fathers, who sailed to America, came from the Bawtry neighbourhood. Stiff penalties were given to clergymen who would not conform; Ezekiel Rogers of Rowley, East Yorkshire, was suspended from his clerical duties for refusing to read in church 'the accursed book which allowed sport on God's holy day.' In 1638, he sailed from Hull to Massachusetts and founded the town of Rowley there. A native of Birstall, Henry Burton, who became a London clergyman, was put in the pillory, deprived of his ears, fined £5,000 and imprisoned for some years because he preached two controversial sermons.

Some of the Yorkshire gentry, Sir Hugh Cholmley of Whitby, Sir

Marmaduke Langdale of Holme-on-Spalding Moor, and Sir John Hotham of Dalton Holme refused to pay Ship Money, with the result that the king threatened to hang Cholmley and Hotham. In 1627, Thomas Wentworth of Wentworth Woodhouse was put in prison for refusing to pay a forced loan. Religious trouble was brewing in Scotland too, where an attempt to have the English Prayer Book forced onto the people was rejected and war broke out between the two countries in 1639, forcing the king to come to York, which was the base for operations against the Scots. During his stay he kept the Maunday Thursday festival in the *Minster*. Having spent a month in York, the king and his nobles at the head of his army marched towards Scotland. On his approach the Scots laid down their arms and swore allegiance. The following year, when the king had disbanded his army, the Earl of Leven and the Marquis of Montrose entered England at the head of a Scottish army, on hearing of which the king left London and came again to York, where he summoned all the peers of England to a great council. Known as the Long Parliament, it assembled on November 3rd. The members reversed sentences on John Hampden, who had instituted the emigration project, and others; obtained the king's assent to their bill for triennial parliaments; procured the abolition of monopolies; and an answer from Charles relative to his method of raising monies by forced loans, tonnage and poundage, Ship Money, etc. They sent commissioners into the counties 'for the defacing, demolishing, and quite taking away all images, alters, or tables turned alterwise, crucifixes, superstitious pictures, monuments, and reliques of idolatry, out of churches and chapels.'

At first when he visited York, the king stayed at the *King's Manor House,* but he enjoyed strolling through the extensive grounds of Sir Arthur Ingrams mansion, which occupied the space between the north side of the *Minster* and the City Walls. Later Charles would stay in Sir Arthur's more comfortable mansion.

A campaign against Scotland, to be led by Algernon Percy, Earl of Northumberland, was planned, but because of Percy's illness it was headed instead by Thomas Wentworth. It was a ragged army consisting of pressed men, poorly mounted and badly disciplined. Some of the Yorkshire gentry signed a petition to the king, protesting at having troops billeted on them, and that the former campaign had cost them £100,000. Among those who signed were Thomas Fairfax of Denton, John Savile of Lupset, Thomas Belasyse of *Newburgh Priory*, John Hotham of Dalton Holme, John Ramsden of Byram, Francis Wortley of Wortley, Philip Wharton of Healaugh, Thomas Mauleverer of Allerton Mauleverer, Hugh Cholmley of Whitby, Walter Strickland of Boynton, Philip Stapleton of Wighill and Warter. Thomas Wentworth, Lord Stafford, told them that to resist a Scottish invasion Yorkshiremen were 'bound by the common law of England, by the law of nature, and by the law of reason.' The colonels of the Train Bands refused to call out their men unless a fortnights pay was given in advance. In the end it was decided to negotiate with the Scots.

A declaration of grievances, known as *The Remonstrances*, was drafted by the Long Parliament and it caused a constitutional crisis which led to the Civil War.

HOSTILITIES BEGIN

UNDER the pretext of taking her ten years old daughter, Mary to Holland; the princess being betrothed to the young prince of that country, Queen Henrietta Maria set sail from Dover on February 24th, 1642. The real object of the queen's mission, however, was to pawn some of the crown jewels in exchange for arms and ammunition.

The following month Charles moved the Court to York. The Royal printing press was set up in *St.William's College*, under the supervision of the king's printer, Robert Barker. From there propaganda was published in the form of thirty-nine tracts addressed to the royal supporters. Charles's first concern was to get his

3

hands on the vast store of ammunition which was kept at Hull in great magazines within the fortress. These arms consisted of all the ammunition levied against the Scots. With this object in view he travelled to the port in person with 300 horse, required Sir John Hotham, the governor, who had received his commission from the Parliament, to deliver up the possession. Sir John, perceiving that matters were drawing towards a crisis, shut the gates and refused to admit the king, although he requested to enter with twelve persons only. Hotham, in his report, said :

I had that place delivered me under that sacred name of trust. I could not satisfy him without incurring to me and my posterity the odious name of a villain and faithbreaker. Nothing I could say could give any satisfaction to His Majesty and some of His Majesty's train with great earnestness cried out to kill me and throw me over the wall.

Charles proclaimed Hotham a traitor and after waiting twelve hours in vain, rode off to Beverley. During his stay in Beverley, Charles lodged at a house near the North Bar Within.

On July 7th, the king advanced to Beverley with 3,000 foot soldiers and 800 cavalry and marched towards Hull. On hearing of the king's approach, Sir John Hotham determined that the surrounding country should be laid under water. The sluices were immediately pulled up and the banks of the Humber cut, so that the next day by the aid of the spring tides, the meadows and pastures to the extent of two miles on every side of Hull were inundated with water. A sortie made by Hotham almost captured the king, who soon resolved to raise the siege and clear off his forces. Being pursued by Hotham's troops, Charles found shelter in the old brick manor house, known as *Hall Garth* and standing on the south side of the *Minster*.

Let us pause for a moment to examine the loyalties of the Yorkshire gentry. Ranged on the side of Parliament were Ferdinand, second Lord Fairfax,and his son Thomas Fairfax. Lord Ferdinand was the son of a brave and gallant soldier, Thomas Fairfax of Denton, who was created Baron Fairfax of Cameron, in

4

the Peerage of Scotland. He died in 1640 at the age of eighty and was buried in the church at Otley. He was succeeded by his son Ferdinando, one of seven sons. Sir Thomas was knighted by King Charles I on the disbandment of the Scottish army. The youngest of Ferdinand's sons was Colonel Charles Fairfax, who brought up his fourteen children at *Menston Hall.* The others were Sir Algernon Percy of Northumberland; Edmund Sheffield, Lord of Mulgrave; Philip, Lord Wharton of Healaugh, a strong Presbyterian; Charles Howard and his father Edward, Lord Howard of Escrick; Sir Philip Stapleton of Wighill and Warter, a prominent Presbyterian ; Sir John Hotham of Fylinghall, and his son also John; Sir Matthew Boynton of Barmston; Sir Thomas Mauleverer of Allerton Mauleverer, Knaresborough; Sir William Constable of Flamborough and Holme on Spalding Moor; Sir John Danvers of *Danby Castle;* Sir Richard Darley of Buttercrambe; Richard Dean, who was born near Leeds; Isaac Evre [or Eure] ; John Lambert of *Calton Hall,* Kirkby Malham; Francis Lascelles of *Stank Hall,* Northallerton; Sir Henry Vane; Thomas Norcliffe of Langton, who married a daughter of Sir Thomas Fairfax; and the following members of Parliament who played a prominent part : John Alured, Hedon; John Anlaby, Scarborough; James Chaloner, Aldborough; Thomas Chaloner, Richmond; Henry Darley, Malton; Alderman Peregrine Pelham, Hull; and Adrian Scrope, Ripon, Bristol and Lyme Regis.

On the side of the king were : Thomas Wentworth, Earl of Stafford; Thomas Belasyse; Lord Fauconberg of *Newburgh,* and his son John; Sir Marmaduke Langdale; Sir Francis Wortley; Sir John Ramsden of Byram; Sir Richard Graham of Norton Conyers; Sir John Mallory of Studley; Sir Philip Monckton of North Grimston; Sir Thomas Danby of Danby Wiske, M.P. for Richmond; Sir William Vavasour of Hazelwood; Sir Henry Slingsby of *Red House,* Nun Monkton and *Scriven Park,* Knaresborough; and Sir Edward Osbourne of Kiveton.

5

Some of the families were divided amongst themselves; Lord Savile was for the Parliament, but his cousin, Sir William was for the king. Hugh Cholmley was for Parliament at first, but his brother, Richard was a Royalist. Of the Mauleverers, Richard was on the side of the king, but Sir Thomas was a Parliamentarian. Sir Walter Strickland of Boynton was an ardent Roundhead, but Sir Robert Strickland of Thornton Bridge was a Cavalier. The barons Evre (or Eure) of Cleveland were Royalists, whereas Isaac Evre was a Parliamentarian.

On June 3rd, 1642, the king addressed more than 40,000 of his supporters on Heworth Moor. Many of them signed a petition begging him to be reconciled with Parliament, but the war began on August 22nd, when Charles raised his standard at Nottingham. It was not until October that fighting broke out in Yorkshire, when on the fourth the younger Hotham led an attack on Cawood Castle, which had been fortified by the Archbishop of York, John Williams and garrisoned by the Earl of Newcastle's famous 'White Coats.' They were driven out by Hotham's men and the Archbishop fled to Wales, where he remained ever after.

The following week Sir Thomas Glenham, the Royalist governor of York Castle, placed a garrison in Pontefract and marched against the West Riding clothing towns, capturing Sir John Savile, who was on his way to join the Fairfaxes who were encamped on Harden Moor, near Bradford. Glenham's forces passed through Leeds to attack Bradford, but they met stiff resistance and were attacked in the rear by young Hotham, who had by then occupied Selby. The Royalists returned to York, while Hotham joined up with the Fairfaxes in Leeds.

Tadcaster became the headquarters for Lord Fairfax, who was now commander-in-chief of all the Parliamentary forces in the north. He had about 1,000 men stationed at Tadcaster, while his son, known as 'Black Tom', held the bridge at Wetherby with 300 foot soldiers and 40 horse. This small force was surprised early one morning by a body of 800 men under Glenham. The guards being asleep at their posts, enabled the Royalists to steal partially into the town without being discovered. The brave Sir Thomas Fairfax, with only four men at their arms, withstood the shock of the enemy and repulsed them, when Major Carr of the Cavaliers was slain. The attack was soon renewed, but in the midst of the conflict Fairfax's magazine was blown up, and produced so tremendous an explosion, that the Royalists, believing that the Parliamentary forces had cannon, began to retreat towards York and were pursued by 'Black Tom' with his small body of mounted troops, who took some prisoners. Sir Thomas lost eight or ten men, of which seven had been blown up with the powder.

Sir Thomas Mauleverer's house at Allerton Mauleverer was plundered in a barbarous manner by the Royalists.

Glenham's men had lost faith in his leadership and the Earl of Newcastle was solicited to take command. On his way south he defeated the young Hotham at Pierce Bridge. Newcastle speedily marched from the north to York with an army of 6,000 men, furnished with ten pieces of artillery, where he arrived on November 30th. Three days later he proceeded with 4,000 men and seven pieces of cannon to attack the Parliamentarians at Tadcaster. Newcastle began the attack at about eleven in the morning and the fighting continued until nightfall, when the darkness compelled them to suspend operations. Under cover of night, Sit Thomas Fairfax withdrew his forces and retreated to Selby and Cawood. According to Lord Ferdinand Fairfax more than 40,000 musket shots were discharged that day, besides the fire from the artillery; but the slaughter bore no proportion to the shot expended as the number killed did not exceed 300. Captain Lister, a valuable officer under Fairfax, was killed in this action.

By the defeat at Tadcaster, the Parliamentary army was cut off from its friends and supplies in the West Riding, for Newcastle's army occupied the towns of Sherburn-in-Elmet, Ferrybridge and Pontefract; however, Sir Thomas Fairfax in a nights march eluded all their vigilance, passed all their posts, and reached Bradford

7

with three troops of horse, 300 foot and some arms in December, 1642.

SIEGES

BEFORE the arrival at Bradford of Sir Thomas Fairfax, a body of the king's forces, numbering about 800 men, were sent from the garrison at Leeds to occupy the town. They encamped at Undercliff, about a mile distant from the town, and from where they marched to the assault; the townsmen met this attack with great resolution and soon caused the assailants to retreat in a great hurry and confusion back to Leeds. On December 18th, the attempt was repeated by a larger force from Leeds, consisting of five troops of horse, six troops of dragoons and 200 foot soldiers, commanded by Colonel George Goring, Colonel Evans, Sir William Saville, and Sir John Goodricke. About 80 of the inhabitants had muskets, the rest were armed with clubs, spits, flails, halberds, scythes, and such rustic weapons. *St.Peter's* church was turned into a fortress, the walls being hung around with packs of wool, while their choicest marksmen were placed on the tower.

The Royalists made repeated attempts to enter the town by storm; but were as often repulsed. About noon, the inhabitants received a reinforcement from Halifax, and determined at once to make a general sally; therefore watching their opportunity, they rushed out of the church, seconded by those in the lanes, and met the enemy face to face. The clubs, scythes and rustic weapons of the townsmen did great execution; and such was their fury that they would neither give nor take quarter. During the heat of this action, a young nobleman, Sir John Hope, at the head of foot, being in advance of his men was taken prisoner, asked for quarter, and was told he should have 'Bradford quarter'; he was instantly slain, and his men seeing the fall of their leader, fled.

At length the Royalists retreated, having had more than 100 men killed and wounded in the contest. On the side of the town, not

St.William's College, York.

The King's Manor House, York.

Cawood Catle (From an old engraving)

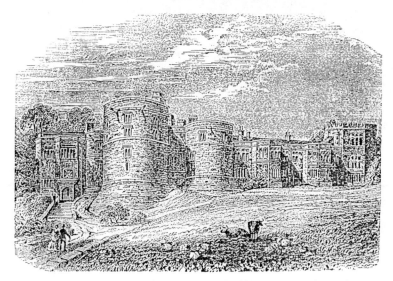

Skipton Castle.

more than five were killed and about twelve wounded.

It was probably in the autumn of 1642 when Henry Clifford, fifth Earl of Cumberland and Lord of the Castle and Honour of Skipton, first garrisoned his castle for defence against the Parliamentarians. The garrison numbered 300 men and the governor was Sir John Mallory, and his lieutenant Major Hughes. The Skipton parish register contains many entries relating to the siege. The earliest are dated December, 1642, and notify the burial of 'souldiers slayne.' Of entries of this sort there are about fifty, extending over the years 1642-8, although a hiatus of three years occurs in the register of burials.

It is tolerably certain that the siege was not for at least the first two years an active one. Very likely the object of the Parliamentary troops was more to prevent depredations by the Royalists upon the surrounding neighbourhood than to institute a regular siege. Nevertheless, sallies were frequently made from the castle, and on several occasions the loss on both sides was considerable.

It is supposed that the cannon of the Roundheads were placed in two positions. That to which tradition has always pointed is the eminence known locally as *Cock Hill,* which afforded a close and uninterrupted view of the castle. The other position is a hill overlooking the fortress on the north, and from that battery the stronghold appears chiefly to have received most damage, for the western portion seems to have been pretty nearly battered down.

Sir Hugh Cholmley of Whitby was made Deputy-lieutenant and Colonel of the train-bands within the hundreds of Whitby Strand, Ryedale, Pickering Lythe, and Scarborough town. During the days of the Short Parliament he was made a Burgess for Scarborough. In 1641, he was re-elected as Burgess to the new Parliament and created a Baronet of Great Britain. Sir Hugh was commissioned by the Earl of Essex to raise a regiment of foot soldiers and to take over Scarborough Castle and hold it for the Parliamentary cause. The castle was at that time in the ownership

11

of a certain Francis Thompson, a Burgher of the town, who was not for handing over the keys too readily, being a Royalist, but finally did so when Cholmley declared he had 'no other end than to preserve the liberty of the subject and to render duties to his majesty.'

At the beginning of 1643, the greater part of Yorkshire, with the capital, York, and the towns and fortresses of Leeds, Skipton and Knaresborough were in the hands of the Royalists. Sir Thomas Mauleverer seized Ripon, where considerable damage was done to the *Minster*. Sir Thomas had raised two regiments at the beginning of the war, one of horse and one of foot, at his own expense and he commanded them as a colonel in the Parliamentary army. The Roundheads showed little respect for 'Popish relics' and destroyed several of the monuments and other ornamental parts of the *Minster*. They treated some of the inhabitants with 'great cruelty.' Sir John Mallory, an active Royalist, then governor of Skipton Castle, at the head of a detachment of the king's horse, surprised Mauleverer's main guard, stationed in the Market Place, and routed the whole of his forces, took several prisoners, and drove the rest speedily from the city.

On January 23rd, Sir Thomas Fairfax determined to attack the garrison at Leeds, and accordingly marched from Bradford with six troops of horse, three companies of dragoons, 1,000 musketeers and 2,000 clubmen. A trumpeter was dispatched to Sir William Savile, requiring the town to be delivered into the hands of Fairfax for the Parliament, to which Savile returned a disdainful answer. The Roundhead general then approached the town on the south-west side, with colours flying, to begin the assault, which commenced about one o'clock in the afternoon; and in two hours the Royalists were driven from their positions and their cannoneers killed. Sir Thomas and his brother Sir William Fairfax, with Sir Henry Fowlis and Captain Forbes, cut their way through all opposition, and entering the town with

12

sword in hand, at the head of their troops, soon got possession of the place, where they found two brass cannon, with a good store of ammunition, and took 500 prisoners, among whom were six officers. There was said to have been about forty slain. Sir William Savile fled and escaped being taken by crossing the river, but Sergeant-major Beaumont was drowned in making the attempt. The following memorandum occurs in the register of Leeds Parish Church :

23rd January 1643 Captain Boswell slain at Seacroft battle, and six soldiers. A gentleman and two common soldiers slain in Robert Williamson's house, of Hunslet : Five more slain - nine more in May ; sixteen more in June ; twelve more in July. 26 soldiers buried July and August 1643.

Guildford Slingsby was in Cleveland, raising troops for the king, but he was defeated at Guisborough by Sir Hugh Cholmley and Sir Matthew Boynton. In a letter to the Speaker of the House of Commons, Lord Fairfax wrote :

Among the prisoners taken by Sir Hugh Cholmley at Malton and here at Guisborough, it is found that a great number are papists ; and indeed the strength of the enemies will be found to consist much of papists and popishly effected ; the Earl of Newcastle granting his commissions for raising men to papists for the most part.

Queen Henrietta Maria met her mother in Holland and spent a year there, during which time she successfully carried out the business upon which the king had sent her. The Dutch Mynheers, grateful to both the king of England and to the exiled Queen-mother of France, for their political existence, did not send Henrietta Maria away empty handed. At the beginning of February 1643, she embarked in a fine ship called the *Princess Royal;* but fierce tempests arose and the north-east gales drove the queen back onto the Scheveling coast. She bore the terrors of the storm with great courage, replying to her ladies when they were panicking and screaming round her : 'Queens of England are never drowned!'

THE QUEEN AT BAY

IT was the intention to land the cargo of weapons at Tynemouth, where the Earl of Newcastle was waiting to escort the queen, but when she eventually reached English shores, followed by Van Tromp's Dutch fleet, the ships were blown off course by strong gales and the point of arrival was Bridlington Quay. The queen had previously sent supplies during the year she spent on the continent. She also sent General James King, who later became Lord Eythin and then chief military adviser to the Earl of Newcastle. Reports vary a little, but it would seem that the queen had to ride at anchor for two days to enable the Earl of Newcastle to catch up with her.

Also waiting at Tynemouth were four Parliamentary ships, commanded by Admiral Batten, and when the intelligence reached them of the queen's arrival at Bridlington, they lost no time in sailing south. In the meantime a troop of 200 Cavaliers appeared on the hills and the ships were unloaded with the arms and ammunition. A letter from an eye-witness described what happened next :

God that was careful to preserve Her by Sea, did likewise continue His favour to Her on the Land : For that night foure of the Parliament Ships arrived at Burlington, without being perceived by us ; and at foure o'clock in the morning gave us an alarme, which caused us to send speedily to the Port to secure our Boats of Ammunition, which were but newly landed. But about an houre after the foure Ships began to ply us so fast with their Ordinance, that it made us all to rise out of our beds with diligence, and leave the Village, at least the women ; for the Souldiers staid very resolutely to defend the Ammunition in case their forces should land. One of the ships did Her the favour to flanck upon the house where the Queene lay, which was just before the Peere ; and before She was out of Her bed, the Cannon bullets whistled so loud about her (which Musicke you may easily believe was not very pleasing to Her) that all the company pressed Her earnestly to goe out of the house where She was ; so that (clothed as She could) She went on foot some little distance out of the Towne, under the shelter of a Ditch (like that of Newmarket) whither before she could get, the Cannon bullets fell thicke about us, and a

14

Sergeant was killed within twenty paces of Her. We in the end gained the Ditch, and staid there two houres, whilst their Cannon plaid all the time upon us ; the bullets flew for the most part over our heads, Some few onely grazing on the Ditch where the Queene was, covered us with earth. [The present writer has seen part of this letter quoted in the first person, purporting to be from the queen to the king.] The bombardment ceased when the Dutch Admiral sent a message to the Parliamentary ships, warning them that if they did not cease firing, he would consider them as enemies and give orders for his own vessels to open fire upon them.

Upon that they staid their shooting, and likewise being ebbing water they could not stay longer near the shore. As soone as they were retired, the Queene returned to the house where She lay, being unwilling to allow them the vanity of saying, They made Her forsake the Towne. We went at noone to Burlington, whither we resolved to goe before this accident and all that day in face of the enemie we disembarked our Ammunition. It is said that one of the Captains of the Parliament Ships had been in the Towne before us, to observe where the Queene's lodging was ; and I assure you he observed it well, for he ever shot at it.

According to another report, the queen, directly she was in the shelter of the ditch, remembered that an old dog named Mitte, which had guarded her chamber for years, was left at the mercy of the Parliamentary bombardment. Despite the remonstrances of her servants, she ran back through Bridlington to her bedroom, caught up Mitte in her arms, and fled back to the ditch.

Van Tromp's ships came up with the tide, but they were too big to enter the harbour. Nevertheless they 'mauled Batten's fleet in the rear.'

A Parliamentary tract of the same time says that when Charles, who was at Oxford, heard of his consorts escape, he is said to have remarked that 'the shipmen did not shoote at her, but onely tryed how neere they could goe and misse, as good marksmen used to do.'

Henrietta Maria, with 500 carts, 1,000 horses, three coaches, eight troops of horse and fifteen companies of foot, began a

15

perilous journey across the Yorkshire Wolds, calling for hospitality at *Boynton Hall,* the home of Walter Strickland. The reception must have been a cool one, for this Strickland was an ardent Roundhead, and it was he who was sent to Holland to complain of the help given to the queen.

Henrietta Maria spent a night at Burton Fleming, where she lodged in the *Old Manor House,* [which is now a farmhouse]; she also spent a night at Malton. Eventually she reached York safely, to stay there for several months and where she won over some new recruits to the king's side, including the Marquis of Montrose and Sir Hugh Cholmley. After the Battle of Edgehill, in October 1642, Cholmley had become certain that there would never be a settlement with King Charles. Disguising himself with a black patch over one eye, he set out from Scarborough Castle to York on March 20th,1643, and sought an interview with the queen. It has been said that when he kissed her hand he changed his allegiance and promised to deliver Scarborough Castle and town to the Crown. Cholmley sent a letter to the Earl of Essex, resigning his commission, but it was intercepted by Sir John Hotham, the governor of Hull. Some wheeling and dealing went on resulting in Hotham releasing one of Cholmley's men, Captain Browne Bushell, who was a cousin of both Cholmley and Hotham, but only on the secret condition that Browne Bushell would take Scarborough back for the Parliament. Late one night, while Cholmley was away at York, Browne Bushell arrived at Scarborough by sea with forty sailors and was admitted to the castle with his brother. They quickly seized the officer in charge and turned the garrison out at the gate. Sir Hugh hurried from York with a strong contingent of Royalist soldiers and parleyed with Browne Bushell at the castle gate. Faced with such odds, Browne Bushell was persuaded to surrender the fortress to Cholmley. A writer of the time stated :

Though able to hold out against an army of 10,000 men was thus twice taken in a week without shedding a drop of blood.

16

Cholmley strengthened the defences of Scarborough Castle with trees from Newton Dale and wood, iron and lead taken from Pickering Castle.

THE BATTLES FOR THE TOWNS AND CASTLES

THE town of Leeds in those turbulent times often changed hands, but was never the scene of much bloodshed. Most of the inhabitants of the clothing towns favoured the Parliament because King James had alienated them by refusing to allow them to export undyed cloth, thereby allowing the Dutch to set up their own looms, causing much loss of business to the Yorkshire weavers.

Lord Ferdinand Fairfax being compelled to retreat from Selby; and Leeds and Bradford being the only places of strength held by the Parliamentarians northwards of Hull, Sir Thomas Fairfax determined to take the garrison of Wakefield, then in the possession of the king's forces, and held by about 300 men; accordingly on the morning of May 21st,1643, he, at the head of 1,100 horse and foot, marched from Leeds to attempt the reduction of that town. The battle commenced about four o'clock in the morning, and after an hour and a halfs hard fighting, Sir Thomas entered the town, took 500 prisoners, with 80 officers, 27 colours, and a large quantity of ammunition. Lord Fairfax wrote to the Speaker of the House of Commons on May 23rd, and after stating that the Earl of Newcastle had occupied Rotheram and Sheffield, continued :

The Earl of Newcastle's army now do range over all the south west part of the country, pillaging and cruelly using the well-affected party ; and here about Leeds, Bradford and Halifax, being a mountainous barren country, the people now begin to be sensible of want, their last years provisions being spent, and the enemies garrisons, stopping all the provisions of corn and flesh, and other necessaries that were wont to come from the more fruitful countries to them ; their trade utterly taken away, their poor grow innumerable, and great scarcity to relieve them ; and this army which now lyes amongst them to defend them from the

enemie, cannot defend them from want, which causeth much murmure and lamentation amongst the people ; and for the army itself, it is so far in arreare, and no way appearing how they shall either be supplied with money or succours as they grow very mutinous. Yet upon Saturday last, in the night, I caused to be drawn out the garrisons in Leeds, Bradford, Halifax and Howley, some horse, foot and dragoons, in all about 1,300 men, and sent them against Wakefield, commanded by my son, and assisted by Major-general Gifford, Sir Henry Fowles, and Sir William Fairfax, with divers other commanders ; they appeared before Wakefield about four o' clock on Sunday in the morning, where they found the enemies (who had intelligence of their designe) ready to receive them ; there was in the town general Goring, Sergeant-major general Mackworth, the lord Goring, with many other principal commanders, and eminent persons, with about seven troops of horse, and six regiments, containing 3000 foot ; the towne well fortified with works and four pieces of ordinance, yet our men, both commanders and common soldiers, went on with undaunted courage, and not withstanding the thick volleys of small and great shots from the enemie so close as they beate quite out of the towne the most part of the horse, and a number of foot, and made all the rest prisoners, and with them took four pieces of ordinance, and all the ammunition then in the towne, and a great number of arms, and amongst the prisoners general Goring himself, with divers other commanders, and other common soldiers, in all about 1500 men, and 27 colours of foot, and three cornets of horse. When the towne was thus taken, they found their number and strength too weak to keep it and their prisoners, so they left the place and marcht away with their booty. In taking the towne, we lost no man of note, and not above seven men in all ; but many of our men were shot and wounded.
Signed *Fer. Fairfax.*

On June 30th, the Earl of Newcastle, with an army of ten or twelve thousand men, advanced towards Bradford for the purpose of punishing the inhabitants for their former disloyalty to the Crown. The Fairfaxes, with a force of only 4,000 men, met the Royalists upon an open plain called Adderton [or Adwalton] Moor, and decided to give battle. The contest was severe and bloody; the Parliamentarians suffering great loss. Casualties were heavy with some 2,000 men killed or wounded on both sides, and that day and the next, about as many of Fairfax's army were taken prisoners. Lord Fairfax fled to Bradford. Sir Thomas, with a small body of horse, escaped to Halifax, but next day he joined his father in Bradford. About 700 Roundheads were slain. 'Hodgson Lane,' Drightlington, is named after a Parliamentary captain. John Hodgson, who marshalled his troops here and made a stand before being scattered. One of the Royalist commanders who distinguished himself in the affray was Sir Philip Monckton, and there is a tablet commemorating him in North Newbald church.

The situation of the Fairfaxes was now most perilous. Sir Thomas had only 800 foot and 60 horse to make the best defence he could against the large force of the Earl of Newcastle. Bradford church and steeple were again manned, and once more the tower was hung round with sheets of wool; the Royalist cannon were soon brought to bear upon it, and with much effect, 'that the shot cut the cords whereon the sheets of wool hung, and down they fell, which the enemy immediately perceiving loudly huzzaed their fall.' Two assaults were made and beaten off; the besieged finding it impossible to defend the place, and not wishing to fall into Newcastle's hands, Sir Thomas with only 58 horsemen charged upon the enemy and sword in hand cut his way through. The wife and children of Fairfax were by his side when he took this dauntless resolution. Lady Fairfax was taken prisoner, but was shortly after sent back to her husband by the Earl of Newcastle in his own coach. Sir Thomas reached Leeds safely, followed by about 80 of the foot who had broken through and arrived mounted on horses which they had taken from the enemy.

Meantime the Hothams at Hull were conspiring with the Royalists to hand over the port, and a message came from that place saying that the citizens would gladly welcome Lord Fairfax as their governor. Accordingly Lord Fairfax and his son set off for Hull. After a most fatiguing march of sixty miles, harassed on

19

Sir John Hotham

Sir Thomas Fairfax

all sides by the Royalists, and a severe skirmish at Selby in which Sir Thomas was wounded, being shot through the wrist, they arrived at Hull in a miserable condition. Sir John Hotham and his son were arrested and sent to London, being subsequently executed on Tower Hill.

After his success at Bradford the Earl of Newcastle established himself at Pontefract and occupied Rotheram and Sheffield, where Sir William Savile was put in charge of the castle. Bradford was sacked by Newcastle's men, and he gave orders that no quarter be given, but there is a local tradition that the people were spared because, as he was sleeping at *Bowling Hall*, his bedclothes were removed by a ghostly lady in white, crying 'Pity poor Bradford !'

On July 26th,1643, Sir John Mallory, the governor of Skipton castle, despatched an assault party under the Lieutenant-governor, Major Hughes and Lord Darcy, to the *Manor House*, at Thornton, Bradford, some six miles distant. The Thornton parish register contains an entry relating to the first struggle for the *Manor House* : Sepult - Tredeeim militres, die Jul. 26th, 1643.

Nearly all Yorkshire was in the Royalist hands, and on September 2nd, Newcastle, (now having been advanced to the status of Marquis), began the siege of Hull. The Royalist army plundered Beverley, where they were said to have got £20,000 worth of plunder. It was at Beverley where Sir Thomas Fairfax met them with a small force, but was driven back, being overwhelmed by numbers. Hull, however, was not so easy to take by land. The Royalist had two huge cannon, named 'Gog and Magog' and nicknamed 'the queen's pocket pistols.' A newsletter of Sunday, September 17th, stated that :

The Lord Fairfax had againe written to the House of his want of money, and signified that the Townsmen hearing that the Scots were coming and that their Town was to be consigned into their hands, were grown so malignant that they would neither billet nor provide for any of his souldiers, so that he much doubted how he should be able to secure the

21

place ; Conforme to which it was certified in some other letters, bearing date from Yorke, that the Lord Marquess of Newcastle had made himself Master of the Sluice, so that the rebels could not drowne the country, as Hotham did upon his Magesties coming thither, and that the Mayor of Hull would not suffer the forces newly raised by the Lord Fairfax to come within the Town, but quartered them within the walls, where they are like to find but ill entertainment, and it was also signified that on this intelligence Sir John Meldrum was to be despatched to Hull to assist Fairfax in that action, but with one penny of money sent to content the souldiers which will contribute very little to their encouragement.

Help came for Fairfax from Lincolnshire when Oliver Cromwell arrived with arms and ammunition and a contingent of the 'New Model Army', consisting of well trained and highly disciplined soldiers. Further support came when Sir John Meldrum marched from the north with 500 Scottish soldiers. One of the huge Royalist guns was taken on October 11th, and the siege was raised the next day. This date is commemorated at Hull with its Annual Fair.

The Scots made an alliance with the Parliament and they joined with 2,000 men, who had come by sea from Hull, in January 1644. The Marquis of Newcastle marched north to meet the joint forces, leaving John Belasyse in charge of York. Sir Thomas Fairfax had gone into Cheshire to oppose the king's Irish allies, but he sent John Lambert into West Yorkshire where he regained Bradford for the Parliament and successfully fought off an attack by Belasyse. Lord Fairfax was still at Hull and he sent out Sir William Constable, who defeated Royalist troops near Driffield and at Malton, taking the town of Scarborough, but not the castle, and making his way to Whitby.

Early in April the two Fairfaxes united their forces at Ferry-bridge and drove the Royalists from Selby, attacking the town on two sides; capturing Belasyse and 1,700 men. Following this victory, Sir Thomas Fairfax was joined by the Scots at Wetherby, under the Earl of Leven, with the united forces to the number of 16,000 foot and 4,000 horsemen; they then advanced to besiege

22

York, which they surrounded except on the north side, on June 3rd. [The present writer has seen the following dates given for the commencement of this siege : April 18th; April 19th; April 22nd; and June 3rd.] The Earl of Manchester with 6,000 foot and 3,000 horse, of the last of which Oliver Cromwell was Lieutenant-general, soon arrived at York to assist the besiegers, and the siege was pushed with vigour. Numerous assaults were made, and bravely repelled; sallies were made by the besieged, in which they were defeated and driven back with great loss; their convoys of provisions were intercepted; batteries were erected from which an almost incessant barrage was maintained; the walls were breached and partially destroyed; mines were sprung with considerable effect, and a scarcity of provisions began to be felt by the garrison and citizens.

The Marquis of Newcastle had sent out most of his horse with Lord Goring to join up with a hoped for relieving force, but was still left with 6,000 foot. Hoping to gain time, Newcastle attempted negotiations for a surrender, but on the condition that he be allowed to march out with all honour and colours flying, but this was refused.

Major-general Lawrence Crawford made a rash attempt to capture the city off his own bat; without consulting his superiors he fired a mine under *Marygate Tower,* outside Bootham Bar, and tried to storm the breach, but was repulsed with loss.

Seeing that matters were drawing towards a crisis, the king sent off a pressing order to Prince Rupert to hasten to the relief of the city. Prince Rupert, of the Rhine, was nephew to the king and had made a sweeping victory at Newark. On the evening of June 30th, intelligence was received by the Roundheads that the prince with an army of 2,000 men was advancing towards the city, and that same night his forces would be quartered in the towns of Boroughbridge and Knaresborough. The information as to the size of the prince's forces was incorrect, as he had about 6,000 foot and 7,000 horse, but on reaching Skipton he had expected to be met by troops from Westmoreland; however, they did not materialise, so he pressed on to reach Knaresborough on that same day.

THE DECISIVE BATTLE

ON RECEIVING news of Prince Rupert's approach, the Parliamentarians raised the siege on York and moved their forces out to meet him, encamping at Marston and Hessay Moors, in the hope of encountering Rupert at Skip Bridge on the River Nidd. Rupert, however, sent a squadron to the bridge and pressed on with the main body of his forces to York by way of Boroughbridge, crossing the Ure and the Swale, on to Brafferton, Tollerton and Overton where he wrested a bridge of boats from the few dragoons who were guarding it. Leaving most of his army just north of York, he entered the city with 2,000 men to meet the Marquis of Newcastle. Rupert was keen to get on with a battle, but Newcastle, now old and tired, urged caution; however, when the prince produced a letter from the king, expressing his wish that they fight, he gave way.

Oliver Cromwell is said to have spent the night in *Long Marston Hall.* Many of the officers were lodged with him. The troops were not so comfortable, for the weather was vile, with rain, sleet and thunder. They were also short of food and water. There is a tradition that the women of the village of Marston carried water in their *piggins,* or milking pails, to the soldiers on the hill top.

According to another tradition, Oliver Cromwell is said to have discussed the plan for battle at *Menston Hall,* the home of peace-loving Charles Fairfax, the uncle of Sir Thomas.

On July 2nd, the Parliamentary leaders held a council of war; the English were for fighting, the Scots for withdrawing, and a withdrawal was decided upon. Part of the army were nearly at Tadcaster when a message was received that the Royalists were marching in great force on to the moor. The whole body of the Roundheads was marched back with all speed and were soon

24

occupying the hill [a slight rise], on the left of the Tockwith road, and the Earl of Leven commenced to marshal his Parliamentary troops in battle array along the side of the hill. The earl was in his sixties and a very experienced campaigner. The whole of the morning was spent drawing up the two armies [The present writer has seen several plans, all different, of the arrangement of the field. The one illustrated is the most comprehensive.] The Royal army occupied the northern side of the road and were stationed behind a ditch. On the extreme left were the cavalry commanded by Tuke; then Lord Byron's Newark horse, backed by Colonel Marcus Trevor and Lord Molyneaux; next was the foot commanded by John Napier and backed by Prince Rupert's horse (known as the 'Bluecoats'); then Lord Eythin's infantry, backed by Sir Thomas Widrington's horse. Also in the centre was the foot commanded by Blackston; to the right were several companies of horse under Lord Goring and Corry, backed by Sir Charles Lucas and Lord Dacre. Straddling Moor Lane was the cavalry of Sir Marmaduke Langdale. Newcastle with his 'White Coats' (so called because their woollen cloth jackets were undyed), was late on the field. The Royal forces faced each other across a ditch in which were four brigades of musketeers, and cannon was planted along its edge.

The Parliamentary forces were lined up as follows, looking at the plan from the left : Cromwell with his model cavalry, known as the 'Ironsides' - a nickname given to them by an admiring Prince Rupert - a troop of horse composed of zealous Puritans who were ready to risk all for God's cause, their motto being 'If God be with us, who can be against us?' Cromwell had raised the troop on the outbreak of the war. They were backed by Sir David Leslie's Scottish horse; then Major-general Lawrence Crawford's foot, backed up by Lord Ferdinand Fairfax's foot; next Robert Baillie's foot, supported by Lord Manchester's foot; finally Sir Thomas Fairfax's cavalry, backed up by the Earl of Eglington's Scottish horse.

To look at the location of the moor today is to see a somewhat different scene, for now it is all cornfields. In 1644 it was mainly open moor, part marsh, part sand, and dotted with bushes. South of the ditch was a hedge of brushwood.

The total number of soldiers varies in reports between 40,000 and 60,000, but it was certainly the largest assembly of the Civil War. Each side had about 7,000 cavalry, but the Parliamentarians were credited with more foot soldiers and guns.

During the afternoon the field pieces played against each other for a while, but with little effect, though it was reported that one shot mortally wounded Cromwell's nephew, Valentine Walton, and killed his horse, whilst the Royalist Sir Henry Slingsby recorded :

The first shot killed a son of Sir Gilbert Haughton, that was a captain in the prince's army ; but this was only a showing of their teeth, for after four shots made they gave over, and, in Marston cornfields, fell to singing psalms.

How goodly a sight, [wrote the Rev.Simeon Ash, Lord Manchester's chaplain], was this to behold when two mighty armies, each of which consisted of above 20,000 horse and foot did, with flying colours prepared for the battle, look each other in the face.

About five o'clock a fearful quietness fell on the moor, as each army waited for the attack to begin. It was about this time that Prince Rupert left York, telling the Marquis of Newcastle that he did not intend to fight that evening. This caused Newcastle to take his time and he stopped his coach some distance from the moor, relaxing with a pipe of tobacco and falling asleep.

At seven o'clock the order by the Earl of Leven for a general advance was sounded, and the Royalists were charged. Down the hillside in brave order marched the Parliamentary forces, the different brigades moving like thick clouds. The line of battle extended for a mile-and-a-half, and amidst shouts of 'God and the King!' from the Royalists, and 'God with us!' by the Roundheadsone of the bloodiest battles ever fought in our country

26

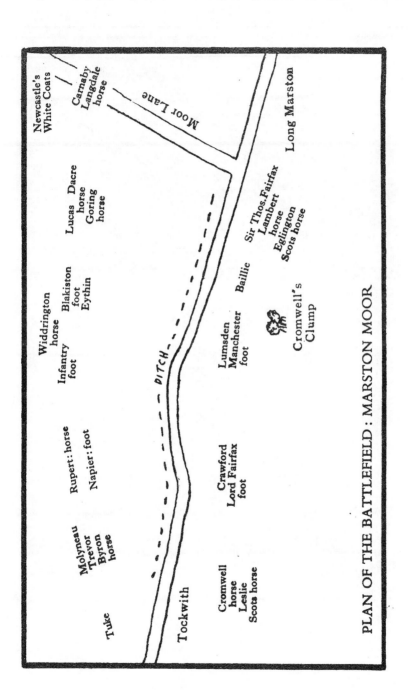

PLAN OF THE BATTLEFIELD : MARSTON MOOR

Long Marston Hall.

Battle Monument, Marston Moor.

was commenced.

Cromwell's cavalry attacked on the west, driving the musketeers from the hedge. Lord Byron then repeated a mistake which he had made earlier at the Battle of Edgehill by riding out beyond the ditch to meet Cromwell, thus positioning himself between his enemy and his own infantry rendering them impotent thereby. Cromwell received a wound in his neck, some say due to a soldier behind him accidentally firing his pistol. Colonel Marcus Trevor claimed he had wounded Cromwell with the point of his sword. Major-general Lawrence Crawford urged Cromwell to leave the field and have his wound dressed. An old cottage at the southern end of Tockwith used to be pointed out as the place where Oliver's wound received attention.

Meanwhile David Leslie with his Scottish cavalry charged Rupert's horse on the right and rear, scattering them.

Prince Rupert had been enjoying his supper and was alerted by the sound of shouting, when he took to the field.

Up Moor Lane Sir William Fairfax led a body of foot. By this time the Marquis of Newcastle had been roused from his slumbers by the sounds of battle and entered the field, encountering Sir William's troops in the lane, subjecting them to a terrible cross-fire and a murderous volley that there was more slaughter here than on any other part of the field.

Sir Thomas Fairfax's cavalry was thrown into great disorder by the furze bushes they had to pass over; however, he placed himself at their head and successfully charged the foe, routing them and chasing them towards York. In this engagement Sir Thomas received a deep sabre cut across his cheek, and was unhorsed, flung to the ground, and wounded on the head and face. Several of his officers were killed, others being fearfully wounded. What was worse Sir Thomas found himself cut off from his own forces and surrounded by his enemy. He narrowly escaped being made a prisoner, saving himself by taking out of his hat the white handkerchief which he had been wearing as a

29

Contemporary woodcut representing Marston Moor after the battle.
Prince Rupert hides in a beanfield. His dog, Boy, lies dead. The
Prince's 'Popish relics' are scattered about the field.

Execution of King Charles I, January 30th, 1649. A contemporary
illustration to a ballad.

badge. [There were no distinctive uniforms for the gentlemen officers at that time; the white handkerchief, or a piece of white card etc, known as a *favour,* was worn in the hat.] By this ruse he was able to join up with Cromwell.

During the time of the aforementioned skirmish a great disaster had fallen upon the remainder of the Parliamentary right wing, where a panic had arisen amongst the newly levied regiments. They were utterly defeated, and horse and foot mingled together madly fled in great confusion, hotly pursued by the Royalists under Sir Charles Lucas and Urry. Elated by the victory, part of the Royalists galloped through the affrighted masses, up the hill side, and commenced the work of plunder at the headquarters of the Parliamentary army. General Goring and Sir Charles Lucas attacked the Scots upon their flank. Twice the Royalists charged and each time were repulsed. Parliamentary reinforcements arrived when a third charge was being made. Sir Charles Lucas was taken prisoner and his men fled towards York. Scoutmaster-general Leonard Watson wrote :

We followed them to within a mile of York, cutting them down so that their dead bodies lay three miles in length.

It was more than half past eight o'clock when the dark squadrons of the Ironsides, having at last extricated themselves from the broken and tangled ground, were seen charging upon Newcastle's flank. In brief space the aspect of affairs changed, and the Royalist infantry was dispersed or slain. But the battle was not yet ended; there was Rupert's triumphant cavalry returned from victorious pursuit, and far more numerous than Cromwell's horsemen to encounter, for the Earl of Leven, thinking the battle was lost, had withdrawn to Leeds earlier. The ranks of the Ironsides, slightly disordered by victory, closed sternly together at the call of Cromwell, and again his piercing tones, echoed by thousands of voices, ran along the line - 'The sword of the Lord and of Gideon!' - and Prince Rupert was literally swept from the field, with frightful carnage, Rupert only escaping by the

31

fleetness of his horse. According to a contemporary pamphlet, he hid in a beanfield, and eventually reached York, where Newcastle and Eythin had also taken refuge.

A fight to the end was endured by the Whitecoats, who refused quarter. They stood their ground in White Syke Close, an enclosure on the moor. Only thirty are said to have survived. Prince Rupert's favourite dog, a spaniel called 'Boy', who was a mascot to the Royalist forces, was found dead amongst the human bodies on that tragic field.

Cromwell, in his letter to the Speaker of the House of Commons, dated July 5th, 1644, wrote :

We never charged but we routed the enemy. The left wing which I commanded being our own horse, saving a few Scots in our rear, beat all the prince's horse. God made them as rubble to our swords ! We charged the regiments of foot with our horse, and routed all we charged ; and of the large army the prince brought into the field I am of the opinion that Rupert has not more than 4,000 men remaining with him.

It was ten o'clock before the battle and pursuit had ended, and the summer moon, as she arose, threw her pale melancholy light on the white death-faces of 5,000 Scottish and Englishmen, slain there by kindred hands. The conquerors had good right to be proud of their dear bought victory; 4,000 or more of their enemies lay slaughtered upon the field; 1,500 taken prisoner, including many men of note, among them Lord Goring; the capture of all the prince's materials of war, consisting of 25 pieces of ordnance, 47 colours, 10,000 stands of arms, two wagons loaded with carbines and pistols, 130 barrels of powder, and all their bags and baggage.

Sir William Ingleby, of Ripley Castle, had taken a troop of horse from his village and was forced to spend the night in gorse bushes near the battlefield. His daughter, who became known as 'Trooper Jane', disguised herself as a man and fought in the battle, receiving wounds. A cousin of Ingleby's, Sir William Waller, who was serving on the Parliamentary side as a commander, suggested that Oliver Cromwell spend the night at Ripley Castle, which was only twelve miles from the battlefield. Cromwell was received aggressively at the castle gatehouse by Lady Ingleby brandishing a pair of pistols, declaring that he was most unwelcome at the castle. After some persuasion she relented and allowed Cromwell to spend the night in the castle library, but sat guard over him all night. When Cromwell departed the next morning he left behind two virtually unused cavalry boots and several executed Royalist prisoners. In the church wall at Ripley are bullet-holes said to have been made by a firing squad of Parliamentary troopers, who lined up against the church wall, a handful of Ripley men who had been taken prisoner. Some of the bullet-holes are high up, as if the firing squad had missed their aim. Some of the troopers had spent the night in the church, where they wrote on a memorial to an earlier Sir William Ingleby: 'No pomp nor pride, let God be honoured.'

One of the many Ingleby family legends asserts it was 'Trooper Jane', who on returning from the battlefield, persuaded her mother to grant hospitality and handed the keys of the castle over to Cromwell, receiving a kiss from him in return. When Lady Ingleby was asked why she had needed two pistols, she replied that 'I might have missed him with the first.'

Sir Richard Graham, of Norton Conyers, a Royalist officer, is said to have fled from the debacle with twenty-six wounds and ridden home, gone up to his chamber on horseback, then expired. The horses hoof-mark is still visible on the stairs. Sir Richard was certainly wounded at Marston Moor, but he did not die until nine years later.

Perhaps the most touching of the many family traditions relating to Marston Moor is the following : Mary, the daughter of Sir Francis Trappes, married Charles Townley Esq., of Townley in Lancashire, who was killed in the battle. During the engagement she was with her father at Knaresborough, where she heard of her husband's fate, and came upon the field next morning to search

33

for her husband's body, while the attendants were stripping the bodies, prior to burial, as was then the custom. She was approached by a general officer, to whom she told her melancholy story. He listened to her with great tenderness, but earnestly desired her to leave the place where, besides the distress of witnessing such a scene, she might probably be insulted. She complied and he immediately called a trooper to escort her. On her way to Knaresborough she enquired of the man the name of the officer to whose civility she had been indebted, and was told that it was Oliver Cromwell.

At a later date relics of the battle were removed to the museum at York. Since the time of the combat Marston Moor has been cultivated, and two centuries later the ploughs were still turning up a bullet, buckle, stirrup, or part of a broken sword. Early in the 19th century the White Syke dike was cleaned out and deepened, when a large number of old-fashioned horse shoes, cannon balls, the blade of a sword lying by the side of its hilt, and other reminders of the conflict, were found. The Moor Lane received a bad name, and tradition states that in the 18th century the villagers were afraid of going there by night, as they met headless horsemen and heard strange cries. Many bullets were also found embedded in the oak trees in Wilstrop Wood when they were felled and sawn up in the 19th century.

In the year 1857, as some navvies were making a drain at a considerable depth through Marston Moor, they cut into a burial pit of the slain of the battle. The foreman of the work said :

We cut twelve yards long and about eight feet wide through the grave, and found most bodies about four feet from the surface, but I consider that we got to the bottom of it, as we took two draws through it after, and the ground below seemed untouched. At one place bodies, about 20 or 25 of them, were laid one over the other in all directions and postures, - the forms of many were left in the clay. At this place there was much of a sort of deposit that looked like soot, not slime, but damp ; the smell at first was intolerable and could be felt at some distance ; it was so bad that the men could only work for short spells. The skulls had preserved

34

their shape, but crumbled away when exposed to the air. There was a bullet in one skull, which dropped out when the skull fell to pieces ; the bones, especially the large ones did not crumble away, but were very brittle when touched with the spade. The teeth were quite perfect, and many of them were taken away by the drainers.

SIEGES AND FALL OF THE CASTLES

WE RETURN now to the time and events immediately following the Battle of Marston Moor. After hiding in the bean field until he felt it was safe to travel, Prince Rupert fled to York, as did the Marquis of Newcastle, Baron Eythin and others. York, however, was no longer a safe refuge so Rupert headed 5,000 horsemen into Lancashire. The Marquis made for Scarborough where he then took ship for the Continent, along with Baron Eythin and Lord Fauconberg. Newcastle's brother, Sir Charles Cavendish also made a hurried departure, leaving his castle at Slingsby unfinished.

Sir Thomas Glenham, the erstwhile governor of York, was once more in charge of the city with a small garrison. On July 4th the siege began and lasted until July 16th, when York was surrendered to Parliament on the most favourable terms to the besieged. On its surrender the Parliamentary generals entered the city in solemn procession and went directly to the *Minster*, where a psalm was sung, and the following day was observed as a day of general thanksgiving. York, thus being subjected to the Parliament, Lord Fairfax was made its governor; and he and his son, Sir Thomas, received communications to reduce all the garrisons in the county that still held out for the king. Sir Thomas gave strict orders that no damage should be done to the *Minster* or any of the churches in the city.

The king's cause in the north was now in tatters, and after a meeting at Ferrybridge, the Parliamentary commanders divided their forces. The Scottish troops marched north to besiege Newcastle. Lord Manchester and Oliver Cromwell went to Doncaster, before moving on the eastern counties. Lord

Manchester sent Lawrence Crawford with a large force to reduce Sheffield Castle, but in order to save great bloodshed, a summons was sent to Major Beaumont, requiring him to surrender it, which was answered with a volley of shot, and a reply that the garrison 'would hold no parley,' and a whole culverin, [a medium to heavy cannon in use in the 16th and 17th centuries], which being brought to the spot, played with such fatal effect, that the garrison was forced to capitulate, and the castle was surrendered to the Parliamentary commander on August 11th. The castle was soon after rendered untenable by order of Parliament.

Tickhill Castle was the next to fall. It was held by a garrison of 'rake belly cavaliers', who were 'exceedingly oppressive' to the country round. Colonel John Lilburne came and took it, against the orders of Lord Manchester, who threatened to hang him.

Helmsley Castle was the property of George Villiers, Duke of Buckingham, and a *favourite* of the king's father. It was held for the Crown by Sir Jordan Crossland. Sir Thomas Fairfax, with 700 foot and 300 horse, marched to Helmsley. 'Black Tom' received a wound in the shoulder during the siege. The Parliamentarians placed their cannon on *Plockwoods Bank,* which is to the south of the castle. Reinforcements for Crossland were sent from Knaresborough, but they were attacked and beaten before reaching Helmsley. The garrison surrendered on honourable terms, including the safe conduct to Scarborough. The Parliament ordered that the castle should be dismantled and one side of the keep was blown to pieces by a terrific explosion.

Late in November, Oliver Cromwell and John Lilburne laid siege to Knaresborough Castle. When it surrendered on December 20th, inside were found four pieces of fine ordnance, a large store of arms, powder and ammunition; a considerable quantity of coin and plate to the value of £1,500, with other valuable booty. Lord Lytton gives a story of the siege :

A youth whose father was in the garrison, was accustomed nightly to get into the deep dry moat, climb up the glacis [an open slope in front of a fortress] and put provisions through a hole where the father stood ready to receive them. He was perceived at length ; the soldiers fired on him. The poor lad was made prisoner, and sentenced to be hanged in quite medieval fashion within sight of the garrison. There was, however, a certain lady who, with great difficulty, prevented the barbarous order from being carried out, and when the castle had capitulated and the soldiers had left the boy was released.

Pickering did not escape from some share of distress. The castle, which was already in a weakened state, for Sir Hugh Cholmley had taken from it wood, iron and lead to Scarborough Castle to build up its defences, suffered a bombardment from the Parliamentary cannon, which must have been placed on *Beacon Hill*, or a neighbouring promontory, for the western curtain wall 'had suffered much injury,' according to a survey carried out by the Commonwealth after the war. Early in the 20th century, a number of cannon balls were found embedded in the bank below the wall. The Parliamentarians, led by Sir William Constable, after a skirmish in upper Boroughgate, [now Castlegate], in the end were the victors. After the castle was taken, great quantities of papers and parchments were brought out and scattered about the streets. The Roundhead soldiers pulled down the beams of at least one house in the castle. Some troops are said to have been quarterd in the Parish Church, and that they smashed the ancient font and tore the church Prayer Book to pieces. The officers were lodged in the *Bay Horse* hostelry.

The first of the three sieges of Pontefract Castle began on Christmas Day of that momentous year of 1644. The castle garrison kept the Parliamentarians at bay for some time, although they were at times reduced to the greatest distress for want of provisions. On January 19th, 1645, after an excessive cannonade against the walls of the castle, the *Pix Tower* gave way, and by its fall carried part of the wall along with it, by which a breach was made; but while the castle was thus assailed the defenders were not inactive. A shot from the fortress struck a match belonging to the Roundheads, and some sparks falling into the powder, it instantly exploded and killed twenty-seven men. By a well-directed fire of musketry, the besieged forced their enemy to keep at a distance, and frequently did considerable execution.

On January 21st, General Sir Marmaduke Langdale, at the head of 2,000 Royalist horse came to the relief of the garrison. Colonel John Lambert fell back, fighting stubbornly and losing some 300 men.

Sir Hugh Cholmley, the governor of Scarborough Castle carried on a protracted negotiation with the Parliament and refused to deal with Sir Thomas Fairfax, insisting instead of communicating with Parliament direct, but all the time procuring supplies of food and materials to face a siege.

In January 1645, a body of 3,000 Scots, commanded by Sir John Meldrum, installed their cannon in *St.Mary's* church and fired at the castle through the great east window. Cholmley was able to hold the town and harbour until February, but after that he was confined to the castle, which received a great battering from Meldrum's ordnance. With Sir Hugh throughout the whole of the operation was his wife, Lady Cholmley. She conducted herself with great composure and bravery, tending the wounded and the many cases of scurvy.

On one occasion Sir John Meldrum sent savage threats to Cholmley, that if his terms were not immediately accepted, he would make a general assault on the fortress that night, and in the event of one drop of his mens' blood being spilled he would give orders for a general massacre of the garrison, sparing neither man nor woman. Sir Hugh made known this threat to his lady, but she implored him to on no account let her peril influence his decision to the detriment of his own honour or the king's affairs.

Sir Hugh accordingly rejected Meldrum's proposals and the garrison prepared itself for the furious attack which commenced on May 11th. While the castle gateway was being pounded, thus occupying the governor, another attack was made on the southern end of the wall towards the sea, and the bloodshed here was

38

greater than that at the gateway. Sir John Meldrum, courageously leading his men, met with a serious accident; he 'had his hat blown off, which he labouring to recover, his coat was blown over his head, and striving to get it down, the wind blew him over, head foremost down the cliff among the rocks and stones at least steeple height.' Although rendered speechless for three weeks, he was up and about in six weeks.

At last the tower of the castle keep was split in two by the onslaught of cannon fire. Stones from the keep were thrown down on the advancing Parliamentary troops and Meldrum received another wound, this time in his thigh, which ultimately proved to be fatal. He was replaced by Sir Matthew Boynton.

When the great keep was destroyed, Lady Cholmley :

Was forced to lie in a little cabin on the ground several months together, when she took a defluction of rheum upon one of her eyes [a watery discharge]. which troubled her ever after and got also a touch of the scurvy then so rife in the castle, and of which it is thought was not well after.

In the end it was famine and illness that ended the siege; with many men suffering the effects of the scurvy, caused by the lack of fresh meat and vegetables. On his forty-fifth birthday, July 22nd,1645, Sir Hugh was forced to come to an agreement with his enemy and honourably surrender the castle. It was a pathetic procession that left the stronghold, for many of the officers were in such a weak condition that they had to be carried out in sheets or helped along between two men.   A Parliamentary officer ironically remarked that "the rest were not very fit to march."

It seems that the women in the castle had threatened to stone Cholmley unless he capitulated. Sir Hugh and Lady Cholmley escaped by boat.

The Moderate Intelligencer, [a newspaper sympathetic to the Parliamentary cause], of July 23rd,1645 announced with great satisfaction :

We heare likewise that *Scarborough* is also yeelded into our hands, Sir Hugh hath none other condition for himself, but with his wife and children passe beyond seas. This is excellent good newes, and is a very terrible blow to the enemy.

Prayers of thanksgiving were offered by Parliament; and the Cholmley properties were sequestrated. His 'great house' at Whitby was pillaged and Roundhead troops were garrisoned there. The privations of the Scarborough siege had weakened Lady Cholmley and shortened her life.

The hill to the south of Scarborough, anciently known as *Weapon-ness,* has been renamed *Oliver's Mount,* based on a local tradition that Cromwell fired his guns at the castle from that height. As we have seen, the cannon were placed in the Parish Church, and there is no evidence that Oliver was ever at Scarborough at all.

Mulgrave Castle, near Whitby, belonged to Edmund, Lord Sheffield, Lord President of the North, whom King Charles I created Earl of Mulgrave. The earl was a keen Parliamentarian and the castle changed hands more than once, while the district suffered severely from the Scottish army.

The second siege of Pontefract had ended the day before Scarborough fell. It had started only three weeks after the first siege, which is why the two are sometimes counted as one. There was, however, this gap of three weeks in March, which gave the castle governor the opportunity to re-provision the fortress in readiness for the new incarceration, which followed on from the departure of General Langdale, when the Parliamentary troops again entered the town and took possession of it. For a period of four months the castle received incessant cannonades, attacks and sorties, the garrison being reduced to a state of famine, forcing the surrender of the castle by a honourable capitulation on July 21st. Sir Thomas Fairfax was appointed governor, but as he was sufficiently committed in the field, he placed Colonel Cotterel in the fortress as his substitute.

40

Sandal Castle, near Wakefield, was held for some time by Colonel Bonivant and an artificial hill, known as *Sandal Castle Hill*, was constructed of principally clay, granite stones, and soil, in order to protect the building from the cannon of the Parliamentary forces who had taken up a commanding position on *Lawe Hill*, Wakefield, upon which they too had raised a mound. It was said that the Sandal hillock was made in a night. The castle, however, was exposed on that side which faced Horbury; and at a place afterwards called *Castle Hill*, in that township, the Roundheads threw up a temporary hill, placed cannon upon it, and commenced firing at the castle before the besieged were aware of what the besiegers had done and accomplished in that direction. They thus affected a breach in the walls. The first cannon ball that entered the building was fired from the mound at Horbury, and this advantage being followed up, led to the surrender of the castle to the Parliamentarians, after an obstinate resistance on the part of the Royalist defenders. A man named Whitehead, holding the position of parish clerk at Horbury, was the cannonier who fired the first shot that struck and damaged the castle. This man never left his duty at the cannon until the siege was finished, and his wife daily carried him his rations from the village. The family of Whitehead, before and after this time, for several generations, had one of its members officiating as clerk at Horbury church.

Many relics of the siege have been picked up in adjoining fields, which were formerly parts of *Sandal Castle Park*. The hill made at Horbury for the occasion was much larger than the mound at the top of *Lawe Hill* and apparently at a nearer distance to the castle. This hill was situated on a piece of table or sort of platform land, very suitable for the purpose it was then used for, and in a commanding position as regarded the operation against the Royalists. It was in existence a long time after the destruction of the castle, but much later it was bought by a Mr Schofield, a solicitor at Horbury, who caused the earthwork etc to be removed.

Castle Bolton, in Wensleydale, which had been held for the king by John Scrope and a party of the Richmond Militia, fell to the Parliamentary forces in the same month. It was ordered by the Parliament to be rendered untenable, but the work was only partially carried out.

Skipton Castle had faced a blockade of three years by the Parliamentary generals Lambert, Poyntz, and Rossiter. The owner, the Earl of Cumberland died at York in 1643 and was buried at Skipton on December 31st, 'amid the thunder of cannon and the clang of arms.'

The castle was often a place of refuge for beleaguered garrisons as well as defeated regiments of Royalists. Upon the surrender of York Castle, for instance, in the summer of 1644, the garrison withdrew 'with arms in their hands, drums beating, and colours flying, to Skipton.'

The local register contains several entries relating to the flight of the Royalist forces survivors after the Battle of Marston Moor.

Towards the end of 1644, the Skipton Royalists seem to have been more than usually active, for the chronicles tell us that 'scarcely a day passed but information was received [by Parliament] of irreparable depredations committed by parties from Skipton and Knaresborough.' General Lambert, however, was ever on the alert. John Vicars, the Roundhead chronicler, recorded at the close of September :

An account was received from the north that Colonel Lambert, that valiant officer, had taken a troop of horse in Craven.

From the spring of 1645, the siege of Skipton Castle became closer and closer. On February 17th, a daring sally was made. Taking advantage of the absence of the officer in command, Colonel Brandling, Sir John Mallory, the governor of the castle, despatched a force of 150 men under Major Hughes, to the Parliamentary camp at Keighley, which they took by surprise. They captured a hundred prisoners, and possessed themselves of sixty horses and a large quantity of booty. But their victory was short-lived for General Lambert was not far away, and hearing of the reverse the Roundheads had suffered, he hastened in pursuit of the victors, who had begun their homeward march. Lambert overtook them, and after a desperate engagement, in which many were killed on both sides, utterly routed them. Having recovered the spoil taken from the Keighley camp, and liberated the Parliamentary prisoners, Lambert returned with a portion of his troops to camp, while the remainder pursued the defeated Royalists up to the very gates of Skipton Castle. Major Hughes, the commander of the luckless expedition, was killed. His burial was thus noted in the Skipton register :

Feb. 19 - Major Hughes a most valiant souldier.

The king, having constituted secretary Lord Digby Lieutenant-general of all his forces north of the River Trent, his lordship advanced by the route of Doncaster towards York. On his arrival at Sherburn-in-Elmet, he stopped to refresh his troops, when information reached him that Colonel Copley, an officer in the service of Parliament, was advancing with a body of his troops. Digby presently 'summoned to horse', and marched with a party of his troops out of the town to meet his enemy, whom he fell upon and put to flight. Copley's discomfited followers fled through Sherburn, *pell mell,* when that part of the Royal army which had not been engaged in the fight, supposing that the fugitives were their comrades, and that they had suffered a defeat, mounted their horses and dispersed in every direction. At this critical moment, a troop of the Parliamentary forces which had remained upon the field unbroken, fell upon Lord Digby and those around him, and drove them to Skipton Castle. By this fatal catastrophe, Digby's army, which had raised high expectations, was broken up; his baggage, containing his cabinet papers, fell into the hands of his enemy, to the high gratification of the Roundheads. Sir Richard Hutton, High Sheriff of Yorkshire, who had espoused the Royalist cause, was left dead upon the field.

By the fall of Sandal and Bolton castles, Skipton was the only fortress in the north of England still defended against the Parliamentarians. Driven to extremities, and knowing well the uselessness of further defence, Sir John Mallory early in December signified his desire to capitulate, and on the 26th of that month Parliamment received official 'letters from the north bringing an account of the rendition of the strong garrison of Skipton Castle, in Craven, which had long been besieged by our forces.' The House spoke of this surrender as 'one of the greatest importance,' for the whole of the north of England was reduced to obedience to the Parliament. The conditions upon which the besieged garrison surrendered were most honourable; they surrendered with full honours of war, and withdrew from the castle with matches lighted, bullets in their mouths and banners waving.

THE SECOND CIVIL WAR

BY THE summer of 1646 all the Royalist strongholds had been captured. King Charles took the fatal decision of surrendering himself to the Scottish army. The English Parliament being informed of the king's capitulation, immediately entered into negotiations with the Scots about delivering up their prisoner. An agreement was reached upon the payment of £400,000, the king would be delivered to his enemies. On his surrender, Charles had been taken by the Scots to Newcastle-upon-Tyne, and on his way there lodged in the *Red Hall*, Leeds, so called because it was the first house in Leeds to be built of red brick.

A maid servant of the house entreated him to put on her clothes and make his escape, assuring him that she would conduct him in the dark out of the garden door, into a back alley called Land's Lane, and then to a friends house, from where he might escape to France. The king, however, declined her offer, but with grateful thanks and gave her his garter for a token, saying that if it were never in his power, on sight of the token, his son would reward her. After the Restoration, the woman presented the token to Charles II and told him the story. The king enquired from where she came and if she had a husband, and if so, what was his calling? She replied that she was from Leeds and that she had a husband who was an under bailiff. 'Then', said the king, 'he shall be a chief bailiff in Yorkshire.' The man afterwards built *Crosby House,* in the upper Headrow, Leeds.

John Harrison, a celebrated gentleman of Leeds, obtained permission to present to his majesty during his incarceration at *Red Hall,* a tankard of excellent ale, but the king on opening the lid of the tankard, found instead of the expected beverage, that the vessel was filled with gold, which he immediately contrived with great dexterity to hide about his person. This incident was illustrated in the Harrison Memorial window at *St.John's* church, Leeds, which Harrison built in 1634.

On May 11th, the king dined at *Coxlodge*, Topcliffe on the way to Newcastle.

Among those who went to Newcastle to take the king from his Scottish warders was Sir Thomas Herbert, who had a fine Elizabethan house in The Pavement, York, and later lived at 9,Petergate.

One of the king's resting places was at *Porch House*, Northallerton, and there is a local legend that Charles tried to escape through a window of the house.

The Parliament was now in possession of the supreme power, but when the House, in which the Presbyterian element predominated, wished to disband the army, which was headed by the Independents, the soldiers appointed a council of officers and a body of subalterns and privates called *adjutators*, who declared they would not lay down their arms till the freedom of the nation was established. Oliver Cromwell was at first well disposed towards the king, but soon discovered that Charles was not to be trusted. Fighting again broke out, first with the Royalist party in Wales, but Cromwell soon finished the struggle in that quarter; after which he proceeded against the Scots, who had raised a strong army 'to deliver the king from sectaries.' As Sir Thomas Fairfax, from Presbyterian scruples, declined the command of the expedition against Scotland. Oliver undertook it with eagerness as he believed the Scottish army to be in a weak condition. He defeated them at Preston on August 17th,1649, and was received in Edinburgh as a deliverer.

There was trouble in Yorkshire when Sir Matthew Boynton, the governor of Scarborough Castle, and who had succeeded his uncle of the same name, had difficulty in keeping his troops in order. Parliament, it seems were not much better paymasters than the king for wages remained unpaid. In the July, Boynton, like Cholmley before him, turned his coat and declared for the Crown. For a second time the Roundhead army found itself in the position of having to besiege the castle, this time under the

Scarborough Castle.

Helmsley Castle.

Pontefract Castle before the Civil War.

Pontefract Castle today.

48

command of Colonel Hugh Bethel. This siege was a short-lived affair lasting until December 15th, when terms were made by which the governor, officers, gentlemen and soldiers marched out 'with their colours flying, bandoleers filled, matches lighted, and bullet in mouth,' to a close called *Scarborough Common*, where they lay down their arms.

Pontefract Castle fell back into the hands of the Royalists by subterfuge. Colonel John Morris [or Morrice], had formerly been in the Parliamentary army, but due to his conduct and conversation being so openly bad, no commission was given him in The New Model Army, although Cromwell and Fairfax could not but admire the many daring and courageous deeds he had performed in the Roundhead service. Secretly he planned his revenge by changing his allegiance to the Royalist cause. Morris developed a friendship with Colonel Cotterel, who may have been an old companion in arms. Certainly Morris seems to have had free access to the castle, even to the extent of going there to sleep in the deputy-governor's quarters. The garrison at that time only consisted of about one hundred men, and some of these were quartered in the town. Morris, when staying all night at the castle, would frequently get up in the night and go the round of the castle, reporting to the deputy-governor if he found any of the sentinels insufficiently vigilant. He told Cotterel that he had fifty stout fellows true to the Parliamentary cause and who would, when required, throw themselves into the castle, and do their utmost in its defence. By such means as these, Morris gained the confidence of Cotterel, who must be blamed for what followed, as General Poyntz had warned him against Morris. When out of the castle Morris carried on the same game of duplicity, mixing freely at the markets and fairs of the neighbouring towns with men of all parties; and what information he collected that could be of use to his Royalist friends was transmitted to them. Morris succeeded in corrupting four members of the Parliamentary garrison, and who entered into his plan for the surrender of the castle. These

49

were Major Ashby, Ensign Smith, Sergeant Floyd and a corporal. The first attempt was a scaling of the walls, but this plan was foiled by the corporal getting drunk and some guards raised the alarm when the raiding party were spotted. Colonel Cotterel had given orders for some beds and some provisions out of the country to be brought to the castle to accommodate the troops who had been billeted in the town, and whom he now ordered back to the castle.

On June 3rd, Morris accompanied by nine Royalist officers, disguised as peasants, having pistols concealed beneath their clothing, appeared at the castle gate with carts laden with provisions, beds, etc. The drawbridge was lowered and the beds etc were delivered to the main guard. Money was then given to the soldiers to fetch some ale, in whose absence, Morris and his party attacked the main guard, making way for their confederates to enter. They made Colonel Cotterel a prisoner and soon made themselves masters of the castle, after which they were joined by 30 horse and 500 foot, part of the king's shattered troops, when Sir John Digby was made governor. The Royalists now being in possession of the castle, their friends flocked from all quarters and there was soon a powerful garrison, and more than a week elapsed before any number of troops of the Parliament could be got before its walls, they had every opportunity to repair the fortifications and stocking the castle with provisions.

Sir Henry Cholmley was appointed to take command of the siege, but, making only indifferent progress, General Rainsborough was deputed to take his place. Towards the end of October, four Royalists gained entry to the quarters of Rainsborough, who was lodging in the town, by the pretence of delivering a message from Cromwell. Their intention was to kidnap him in exchange for Sir Marmaduke Langdale, who was believed to be imprisoned in Nottingham. However, the general put up a strong resistance and his abductors murdered him.

Oliver Cromwell came to take charge of the siege, but was only there for a month being called to Preston to face the Scottish army. Colonel Lambert then took charge of operations at Pontefract. The Royalist cause becoming more hopeless with every day throughout the country, and the garrison being reduced from 500 to 100 men, with many of these being unfit for duty, were compelled to negotiate with Lambert, who told them he could only act upon his instructions wherein one of the conditions would be the exception from mercy of Colonel Morris, Lieutenant Austwick, and Cornet Blackburn, (these three having been involved in the murder of General Rainsborough), and Major Ashby, Ensign Smith and Sergeant Floyd (the three traitors who had been confederates of Morris in the surprise capture of the castle). Lambert conducted himself, as was his wont, with honour, courage and humanity and was the reverse of being anxious for the death of these seven men, and on request of the garrison that he would allow them six days, in which time the excepted persons might escape, he consented. To these terms the besieged agreed, but two days after made a desperate sally from the castle, and though against great odds, Morris and Blackburn pushed their way through the troops, making their escape. They were, however, soon after captured in Lancashire, from where they were attempting to get away by sea. They were taken to York Castle, but made another attempt to get free. Morris had managed, by means of a rope, to slide down the castle wall, but Blackburn, in making the same move, fell and broke his leg. They were both recaptured, as Morris would not desert his crippled friend. They were tried, sentenced to death, and executed on August 23rd,1649, both of them dying with fortitude and resignation.

The siege of Pontefract Castle ended on March 15th,1649, the garrison having first proclaimed for Charles II. Pontefract Castle has the distinction of being the last bastion in England to yield, effectively bringing the second Civil War to a close. The building was demolished by Parliament orders.

THE KING'S TRIAL AND DEATH

WE MUST backtrack a little now, for while the siege of Pontefract was in progress, the king was to meet his doom. On January 19th,1649, the king was brought before the high court to take his trial. His Majesty, conducting his own defence, refused to acknowledge the authority of the court. He appeared four times and was convicted of High Treason, with other crimes, and was sentenced to death. The Death Warrant was as follows :

To Colonel Francis Hacker, colonel Hunks, and lieutenant-colonel Phayr, and to every of them. 'At the high court of Justice for the trying and judging Charles Stuart, king of England, 29th January 1648-9.

'Whereas Charles Stuart, king of England, is and standeth convicted, attained, and condemned of High Treason, and other high crimes, and sentence on Saturday last was pronounced against him by this court, to be put to death by the severing of his head from his body ; of which sentence execution yet remains to be done: These are therefore to will and require you to see the said sentence executed in the open street before Whithall, upon the morrow, being the 30th day of this instant, month of January, between the hours of ten in the morning and five in the afternoon of the same day, with full effect : And for so doing this shall be your warrant. And these are to require all officers and soldiers, and other good people of this nation in England, to be assisting unto you in this service.'

Given under our hands and seals,

JOHN BRADSHAWE.
THOMAS GREY, (Lord Groby)
OLIVER CROMWELL.
(and 56 others)

Among the 56 others were a number of Yorkshiremen, as follows : Jon Alured, a Grays Inn lawyer and M.P. for Hedon in the Long Parliament; Sir William Constable,Bart., of Flamborough and Holme on Spalding Moor. He was later appointed a member of the Council of State of the Commonwealth; Richard Dean, who was born near Leeds. When the war broke out he became a musketeer, but soon rose to the rank of colonel, fighting in many a battle, dictating terms to Lord Hopton at Truro, and enjoying the friendship of Cromwell. Afterwards, under the Protectorate, he became General and Admiral at Sea. Dean was killed in a naval battle with Van Tromp in 1653; Sir Thomas Mauleverer, who was created a baron in 1641 of Allerton Mauleverer, near Knaresborough; Peregrin Pelham, a Hull alderman and mayor in 1649, also recorder and M.P. for Hull in the Long Parliament; and Adrian Scrope, the grandson of John Scrope of Spennythorne and Danby upon Yore. He was a colonel in the Parliamentary army, and at one time Governor of Bristol. He was M.P. for Ripon in 1622, Bristol 1628, and Lyme Regis 1635-47. Scrope was a barrister-at-law; a baron of the Exchequer, Scotland 1608; Keeper of the Great Seal in Commission 1610, and Joint-Secretary of the Treasury, 1622.

Other Yorkshiremen present at the trial of the king were : John Anlaby of Scarborough, who was one of the persons named as judges of the king. He attended the trial on only one day, but did not sign the death warrant. He was M.P. for Scarborough in 1647, Bailiff of Scarborough 1652, and was elected one of the eight county members for Yorkshire in 1653; Sir John Bouchier, a member of the family of the Barons Bouchier, earls of Eure (Normandy), earls of Essex and Bath, and of the Vale of York. He was a Recruiter M.P. for Ripon in the Long Parliament and took an active part in the war; James Chaloner, the brother of Thomas, listed above, an antiquary and topographical writer and Recruiter M.P. for Aldborough in the Long Parliament and a member of the High Court of Justice; Sir John Danvers of Danby Castle, Cleveland, who represented Malmesbury in the Long Parliament; Sir Richard Darley of Buttercrambe, a Puritan and shelterer of persecuted nonconformists, and who was one of those proclaimed traitors by the Earl of Newcastle in 1643. He is said to have been one of the king's judges, but this is improbable - the Darley who did sit at the trial being more likely to be his brother Henry, who was M.P. for Malton. Sir Richard may have been nominated, but does not appear to have taken his seat at the court;

53

Isaac Evre, a member of the family of Barons Evre [or Eure], in Cleveland. The other members of his family were Royalists, one of whom was slain in the king's cause at Marston Moor, and another at *Newburgh*. Colonel Evre attained great distinction by his military skill, and was appointed to the guardianship of the king at Carisbrook; Francis Lascelles of *Stank Hall,* Northallerton, who was a colonel in the Parliamentary army, and represented Thirsk as a Recruiter M.P. in the Long Parliament. He was appointed a commissioner of the High Court of Justice, but only sat once. Finally, Sir Henry Vane, one of the leading spirits in the troublesome times of the Commonwealth. During his college days he became interested in politics which eventually led him to firm republican principles. On the outbreak of the Civil War, he took an active part against the king. However, he opposed the usurpation of Cromwell, who had him imprisoned. He wrote some fanatical books in a perplexing style, which are now almost forgotten.

Sir Thomas Fairfax was not in the court, although his name was read out as one of the judges, prompting Lady Fairfax to cry out from the gallery that 'he was not such a fool as to come here today!' [It has been written that Lady Fairfax hid behind a mask while she was in the courtroom and that she also shouted 'Oliver Cromwell is a rouge and a traitor!' After a further interruption, Colonel Daniel Axtell ordered the soldiers, 'Fire - fire into the box where she sits!', whereupon the lady rose and quitted the gallery.]

It is known that Sir Thomas Fairfax was against trying the king from the outset.

King Charles's execution took place on January 30th,1649. He was attended at the last by two Yorkshiremen, Sir Thomas Herbert of York, who accompanied the king on his last walk to Whitehall. Just outside *St.James's Palace* the king paused and gave Sir Thomas his watch as a token of his loyalty. The other man was Captain Basil Woodd of *Conyngham Hall,*

Knaresborough, to whom his majesty gave the Star of the Garter.
Did Andrew Marvell witness the execution ? Marvell, who was
born at Winestead, Holderness, was noted as a poet, scholar,
satirist and pamphleteer and later M.P. for Hull. He went abroad
at the outbreak of the war, but came back four years later. In any
event he penned the following moving lines on the death of the
king :

> He nothing common did or mean
> Upon that memorable scene ;
> But with his keener eye
> The axe's edge did try ;
> Nor call'd the gods with vulgar spite
> To vindicate his helpless right ;
> But bow'd his comely head
> Down, as upon a bed.

THE AFTERMATH

OLIVER CROMWELL now dominated the political scene in England. With the aid of John Lambert, he formed a constitution called the *Instrument of Government,* by which the Protector, with his council was invested with the power of peace and war. Cromwell made peace with Portugal and turned the resources of the state to the enlargement of its navy and commerce. He reformed the system of representation to the House of Commons. Small boroughs were disenfranchised and the number of county members were increased. Very few unrepresented towns had yet grown in importance. Of those towns the most considerable were Manchester, Leeds and Halifax. Representatives were given to all three.

Under no English government since the Reformation had there been so little religious persecution. One Yorkshireman who suffered for his religious beliefs was James Naylor of East Ardsley. During the Civil War he had fought for Parliament. He was converted by the preaching of George Fox, the founding Quaker, but soon Fox turned against him and his followers. Of Naylor's preaching during the Battle of Dunbar, an officer who heard him said that he was more terrified by the sermon than by the battle. His views were extreme and some of his followers believed he was Jesus Christ, causing him to change his name from James to Jesus. Naylor was tried for blasphemy; after being whipped and pilloried in London, he had his tongue bored and his forehead branded with a 'B' (for blasphemer). The sentence was to be repeated in Bristol. He refused the aid of a doctor, declaring 'God is my Physician and I need no other.' He was imprisoned for two years. After his release, on his way home to Yorkshire in 1660, the unfortunate Naylor was set upon by highwaymen and so badly cudgelled that he died shortly after.

Oliver Cromwell died on September 3rd, 1658, in his sixtieth year. It seems unfortunate that the Protector had the power to name his own successor. Henry Ireton, the man Oliver most feared, was already dead and the lot fell on Richard Cromwell, Oliver's eldest son, a man completely different in character to his father. Being a Pacifist he did not have the army to back him. He was unable to sustain the Commonwealth and the monarchy was restored in the person of Charles II, in 1660.

It was not long before the Royalists began to wreak their revenge on the Parliamentarians. What was the fate of our Yorkshire regicides? James Chaloner was condemned to death, and reprieved when the rope was placed round his neck, but he died of poison during the same year, in the *Tower of London*. His brother, Thomas, was on the list of those excepted from pardon, but saved his life by escaping abroad, and died in Middleburg, New Zealand. Richard Dean was killed in a naval battle with Van Tromp in 1653. He was buried in *Henry VII's Chapel*, Westminster, but after the Restoration his remains were disinterred, contemptuously dragged through the streets and cast into a pit. General Lambert was brought to England, along with Sir Henry Vane and tried in June 1662; and on July 25th a warrant was issued to the Governor of Guernsey to take into custody 'the person of John Lambert, commonly called General Lambert, and keep him a close prisoner, as a condemned traitor, until further orders.' He died in the severe winter of 1683. Sir Henry Vane was proceeded against as a regicide, was found guilty and beheaded on *Tower Hill*. Adrian Scrope was executed at Charring Cross in 1660. Sir William Constable died before the Restoration and was buried in *Westminster Abbey;* but his body was exhumed after that event, dismembered and cast into a pit. Francis Lascelles was the most fortunate, for he escaped further punishment than a fine of one years income and a dismissal from the House of Commons, with disqualification from holding any office of State.

John Alured died before the Restoration, having retired to Beverley, where he had some property, which was subsequently confiscated by attainder. Sir John Danvers died in 1659, before

Newburgh Priory : Cromwell's final tomb ?

Oliver Cromwell.

the Restoration, as did Isaac Evre, Sir Thomas Mauleverer and Peregrine Pelham.

Sir Thomas Fairfax had pressed General Monk to declare for the Restoration of the monarchy and it was Fairfax who was chosen as the head of commissioners of the two houses of Parliament to see the exiled King Charles II at the Hague. His father, Ferdinand, had died in March, 1647, when Thomas became Baron Cameron. He spent his last seven years crippled by disease, but otherwise seemingly peacefully, at *Nun Appleton Hall,* near Bilbrough, and was buried in the village church in November 1671.

Other individuals suffered harassment over quite some time. Captain Hodgson, a Parliamentary officer, of *Coley Hall,* near Halifax, who wrote his own memoirs, complained that he had been arrested on several occasions, the last one being on September 11th,1662.

Oliver Cromwell had been given the full honours of a State Funeral and was interred in *Henry VII's Chapel, Westminster Abbey.* On January 29th,1661, the bodies of Cromwell, Henry Ireton and John Bradshaw were exhumed and dragged through the streets to Tyburn where they were hanged for a while, then cut down and their heads and fingers chopped off. The bodies were buried beneath the gallows, and the heads were stuck up on poles outside *Westminster Hall.* The final fate of Cromwell's body is the subject of rumour and mystery and different stories have circulated regarding the ultimate destination of the remains. The head has been accounted for, but the most likely tradition regarding the corpse is as follows : Mary, Cromwell's third daughter, had married Lord Fauconberg of *Newburgh Priory.* the story goes that she paid some men not to bury the body in the pit, and that it was taken at night to *Newburgh.* Certainly there is a peculiar vault in the house which had a small metal plate on which was written:

In this vault are Cromwell's bones, brought here, it is believed by his daughter Mary, Countess of Fauconberg, at the Restoration, when his remains were disinterred from Westminster Abbey. 'R.I.P.'

Relics of Cromwell were kept at *Farnley Hall*, between Leeds and Bradford, in the form of his watch, sword and the broad-brimmed hat he wore at Marston Moor; and a table at which he had dined. *Farnley Hall* was the home of the Fawkes family, and also contains some Fairfax relics.

So passed a unique period in our countrys history, after which the Crown was never to have the same power as before the days of the Commonwealth.

LOCAL & REGIONAL HISTORIES BY KEITH SNOWDEN

KINGS IN RYEDALE
Covers 2,000 years of Ryedales association with royalty.
A delightful volume of which he can be justifiably proud.
Nicholas Rhea, *Darlington & Stockton Times.*
AUTHOR'S FIRST EDITION. £1.95. Post 31p.

PICKERING THROUGH THE AGES, The Second Edition.
Now revised and enlarged, with extended text and
many more pictures. Tells the story of the town from its
foundation in pre-historic times to the present day.
£2.55. Post 40p. ISBN 0 9527548 2 7.

HELMSLEY & KIRKBY THROUGH THE AGES
Here is the story of these two ancient Yorkshire market
towns and the many famous people connected with
them.
£2.85. Post 40p. ISBN 0 9514657 4 0

MALTON & NORTON THROUGH THE AGES
The story of these ancient sister towns, their noble
owners and famous sons.
REVISED EDITION. £2.85. Post 40p. ISBN 0 9514657 3 2

THORNTON DALE THROUGH THE AGES
Here is the story of one of Yorkshires prettiest villages and
the famous people connected with it.
£2.70. Post 40p. ISBN 0 9514657 0 8.

SCARBOROUGH THROUGH THE AGES
The story of the Queen of English Watering Places.
REVISED & ENLARGED EDITION.
£2.95. Post 40p. ISBN 0 9514657 9 1.

THE CIVIL WAR IN YORKSHIRE
An account of the battles and sieges and Yorkshires
involvement. One of our best-sellers.
£2.95. Post 40p. ISBN 0 9514657 6 7.

KATHARINE PARR OUR NORTHERN QUEEN
The life and Northern associations of the last wife of King Henry VIII. A unique biography.
£2.95. Post 40p. ISBN 0 9514657 7 5.

MOORLAND MEMORIES
True tales from the Whitby and Pickering Moors.
AUTHOR'S EDITION. £2.85. Post 40p.
ISBN 0 9514657 8 3.

GREAT BATTLES IN YORKSHIRE
Recounting the many battles on Yorkshire soil from the Romans to the Roundheads.
NOW REPRINTED. £2.95. Post 40p.
ISBN 0 9527548 0 0.

A BOYHOOD PICKERING
Keith Snowden recalls living in the Twenties and Thirties, his school activities and life in wartime Pickering. This is social history in a autobiographical style.
£2.85. Post 40p. ISBN 0 9527548 2 7.

THE HOUSE OF YORK AT WAR
A Yorkist account of the Wars of the Roses.
AUTHOR'S EDITION. £2.95. Post 40p.
ISBN 0 9527548 3 5

THE ADVENTUROUS CAPTAIN COOK
The life and voyages of James Cook, R.N.,F.R.S.
Here is the life of this great Yorkshire-born navigator and his exciting voyages of discovery.
£2.99. Post 40p. ISBN 0 9527548 4 3.

ON SALE IN LOCAL BOOKSHOPS, OR DIRECT FROM THE PUBLISHER : CASTLEDEN PUBLICATIONS,
11 Castlegate, Pickering, North Yorkshire, YO18 7AX.
Telephone 01751 476227.
Post free on five or more copies.